DK

ANNABEL KAR

Find out what I make
with these ingredients
on pages 34-35

Mummy and me
COOKBOOK

DK

LONDON, NEW YORK,
MELBOURNE, MUNICH, and DELHI

Design Rachael Foster, Hedi Gutt
Project Editor Carrie Love
Photography Dave King
Food stylists Libby Rea
and Katie Rogers

Publishing Manager Susan Leonard
Category Publisher Mary Ling
Production Editor Sean Daly
Jacket Designer Hedi Gutt
Jacket Editor Mariza O'Keeffe

First published in Great Britain in 2008 by
Dorling Kindersley Limited,
80 Strand, London, WC2R 0RL
Penguin Group (UK)

Text copyright © 2008, 2013 Annabel Karmel
Layout and design copyright © 2008, 2013
Dorling Kindersley Limited

003 – MD424 – Aug/13

A CIP catalogue record for this book
is available from the British Library.

ISBN 978-1-4093-4148-2

Colour reproduction by MDP, UK
Printed and bound in China by
South China Printing Co. Ltd.

Discover more at
www.dk.com

Contents

Introduction

Cooking is great fun. The best way to learn is by watching your Mum or Dad but here are a few tips to help you make the recipes in this book.

When you have tried out the recipes, it's a great idea to invite a group of friends over for a cooking party where you make a meal together. You could even have your own restaurant at home – write out a menu, take orders, and serve a meal to the grown-ups. Or how about you and your guests preparing the yummy treats for a birthday party? Enjoy making the recipes, but most of all... enjoy eating the food!

Annabel Karmel

Kneading dough

To knead, use the heel of your hand to squash the dough away from you. Then fold the top end over toward you and give the dough a quarter turn clockwise. Keep going until the dough turns smooth and silky.

Grating and crushing

Grating cheese
Run a block of cheese down the side of the grater. Grate Parmesan against the small holes and Cheddar on the bigger holes.

Be careful of your fingers!

Grating ginger
Scrape off the skin with the tip of a teaspoon, then grate against the small holes. It's easier if you freeze the ginger first.

root ginger

Crushing garlic
Bash the garlic so it's easy to peel, then crush it with a garlic press or the back of a teaspoon.

Eggs

Eggs come in different sizes and I usually use the medium size in my recipes. When cooking with eggs, it's best to use them at room temperature.

Transfer the yolk from...

TAP TAP

one half shell to the other

letting the white run out

Separating an egg is easy once you know how.

Have 2 bowls ready. Tap the egg firmly on the edge of one bowl so the shell cracks open. Let the egg white drop into one bowl and then tip the egg yolk into another bowl.

soft peaks

stiff peaks

overbeaten

Whisking egg whites

is easiest using an electric mixer (which needs Mum or Dad) but try with a hand whisk.

There are 3 stages to whisking egg white. At the first stage, the whites form soft, floppy peaks when the blades are lifted up. Carry on whisking and they will form stiff peaks that stand straight up, perfect for meringues. If you whisk the egg for too long it becomes lumpy and overbeaten.

Using ring moulds is a good way to make

my mini lemon cheesecakes, as it shows the layers. Before using them, lightly grease the insides as this makes the cheesecakes easier to release.

Removing the ring

Run a knife around the inside edge to release the cakes. It helps if you rinse the knife in cold water after removing each cheesecake.

Melting chocolate

To do this on the cooker, put a bowl over a pan of hot water, making sure the bowl doesn't touch the water. Leave for a minute then stir until all the chocolate has melted. Keep at room temperature.

Things you will need...

Do you recognize all the things in this picture?
You will be using them to make these recipes.

Oven temperatures are given in °C, °F, and Gas Mark.

For fan-assisted ovens, reduce the temperature by about 15°C (25°F).

To preheat the oven, allow at least 10 minutes for it to reach baking temperature.

...an apron

You're bound to get sticky hands but try to keep your clothes clean by wearing an apron.

egg whisk

melon scoop

hand beaters

small sieve

blender

clingfilm

baking parchment

aluminium foil

small saucepan

big sieve

mixing bowls

electric hand mixer

ice-lolly mould

20 cm (8 in) baking tray

ring mould

rolling pin

lemon squeezer

cookie cutters

ice-cube mould

Things to remember

- **Wash your hands** before cooking and when you have been handling raw meat.
- **Wash fresh vegetables** and fruit before you use them in your recipe.

Being careful

- **Hot ovens and hobs** need an adult so just watch or help on these steps.
- **Electrical equipment** and sharp knives must be handled by an adult.

...measuring things

Your number skills will help you to measure out the ingredients. You can use weighing scales, and measuring cups, spoons, and jugs.

Ask an adult to help you grate ingredients.

masher

garlic press

box grater

colander

rolling pin

mallet

wooden spoon

palette knife

whisk

spatula

weighing scales

frying pan

mini-muffin tin

baking tray

chopping board

measuring spoons

measuring cups

piping bag and nozzles

cooling rack

Mini caesar salad

The croutons are so *yummy* that you may want to make double and use the extra ones in soup.

You will need:

For the croutons
- 30g (1 oz) Parmesan cheese
- 2-3 slices of white bread

For the dressing
- $1/2$ small clove garlic (optional)
- 6 tbsp mayonnaise
- $1/4$ tsp lemon juice
- 4-5 drops Worcestershire sauce
- 2 tbsp cold water

For the salad
- 2 hearts of romaine or 4 little gem lettuces, leaves washed and dried.

Makes 4 main-course portions

How to make it...

Ask an adult to help.

1 Grate the cheese

Grate the Parmesan cheese using the fine side of a box grater.

2 Make the croutons

Take 2-3 slices of white bread and cut into small star and heart shapes using mini cutters.

Grill each side for 2 mins

Grill for 4-5 mins

3 Arrange on a tray

Arrange the small bread shapes on a baking sheet, ready to toast under the grill.

4 Sprinkle with cheese

Sprinkle 2 tbsp of the grated Parmesan over the toasted croutons, ready to grill again.

5 Make the dressing

Crush the garlic (see p 4). Put it in a salad bowl with the other dressing ingredients and remaining Parmesan.

Try it...
with chicken

Griddle 2 chicken breasts
that have been marinated
for an hour in olive oil, a
little lemon juice, and a
clove of crushed garlic.
Slice and scatter
over the salad.

or add bacon

Grill 8 rashers of streaky
bacon until crisp. Crumble
and scatter over the salad.

6 Add the lettuce

When the dressing is mixed together, season
with salt and pepper. Then add the lettuce leaves,
tearing the bigger ones into smaller pieces.

7 Mix it all up

Toss the lettuce leaves in the dressing.
Scatter over the croutons and serve.

Lettuce boats

These tasty fillings would also be delicious inside a wrap.

You will need:

- 50g (2 oz) sliced cooked chicken
- 3 tbsp drained, tinned sweetcorn
- 1 spring onion
- 2 tbsp mayonnaise
- 1 lemon
- 4-6 baby gem lettuce leaves

Makes 4-6 boats

How to make them...

1 Tear the chicken

Tear the cooked chicken into little shreds using your fingers. Put in a bowl.

2 Add other ingredients

Mix in the sweetcorn, sliced spring onion, and mayonnaise, plus a little pepper to taste.

3 Add lemon juice and mix

Add a squeeze of lemon juice ($1/4$ tsp) and stir.

Try this Tuna mix

Mix together 2 tbsp mayonnaise, 1 tbsp ketchup and a squeeze of lemon juice. Then add 185g (6$\frac{1}{2}$ oz) drained, tinned tuna (lightly mashed), 2 sliced spring onions, 2 tbsp diced red pepper, and 2 tbsp of drained, tinned sweetcorn.

Try this one too!

Chicken and beansprouts

Mix together 2 tbsp mayonnaise, 2 tsp plum sauce and a squeeze of lemon juice. Then add a handful of beansprouts and 50g (2 oz) sliced, cooked chicken.

4 Fill the lettuce boats

Spoon the filling into nice curly, boat-shaped lettuce leaves.

Make a sail from a napkin and a cocktail stick

Easy cheesy bread rolls

There is nothing like the taste of fresh bread! Bake these *yummy* rolls for your lunch.

You will need:

- 1 x 7g ($^1/_4$ oz) fast-action yeast sachet
- 1 tsp sugar
- 150ml (5fl oz) hand-hot water
- 55g (2 oz) mature Cheddar cheese
- 30g (1 oz) Parmesan cheese
- 225g (8 oz) white bread flour, plus extra for dusting
- $^1/_4$ tsp salt
- 1 tbsp sunflower oil (olive oil is OK)
- 1 egg
- sesame seeds, sunflower seeds, pumpkin seeds, and poppy seeds

Makes 8 rolls (or 16 mini rolls)
Bake at 200°C/400°F/ Gas Mark 6

How to make them...

1 Start with yeast

Put the yeast in a small bowl with the sugar. Add 50ml (3 tbsp) of water and stir to dissolve the yeast. Leave to stand for 5 minutes.

Ask an adult to help.

2 Grate the cheese

Meanwhile grate the Cheddar cheese on the large holes of a box grater, and grate the Parmesan using the fine holes.

3 Mix flour and yeast

Put the flour in a large bowl and stir in the salt. Make a dip in the centre and add the oil and the yeast liquid (this should be frothy).

4 Make into dough

Add the rest of the water and mix to a soft dough. Add a teaspoon of extra water if the dough is dry.

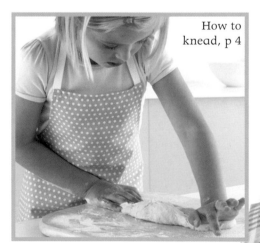

How to knead, p 4

5 Knead until smooth

Turn onto a floured surface and knead until smooth – this will take about 10 minutes. Use the heel of your hand to work the dough.

12

6 Pat dough in circle

Pat the dough out into a circle about 20cm (8 in) across. Spread the grated cheeses over it, then fold the dough in half.

7 Fold in the cheese

Fold in half again, so that the cheese is enclosed. Knead for 1-2 minutes more to work in the cheese.

8 Make into balls

Divide the dough into 8 pieces (or 16 for mini rolls) and form each one into a ball. Put on a lightly oiled baking sheet, about 5cm (2 in) apart, and press down slightly.

⭐ Try this...

Add sliced, sun-dried tomatoes to the dough at step 6. You could also try making some animal-shaped rolls.

Bake the rolls for 12-14 minutes.

Leave to rise

Cover with a damp tea towel and leave in a warm, draught-free place for 40-45 minutes. The rolls are ready to bake when they are roughly double their original size. Preheat the oven after around 35 minutes.

9 Brush with egg

Beat the egg with a pinch of salt. Uncover the rolls and brush the tops with a little of the beaten egg. Sprinkle them with seeds, then put them in the oven.

13

Little pitta pizzas

Everyone loves pizza so why not have a party where the guests design their own pizza faces.

How to make them...

You will need:

- 1 small or half a medium red onion
- 1 tbsp olive oil
- 1 small clove garlic, crushed
- 1 tbsp tomato puree
- 2 tsp ketchup
- 1 tbsp hot water
- 2 small round pittas (or 1 large)
- 50g (1½ oz) Cheddar cheese

Plus toppings of your choice (see opposite for ideas)

Makes 4 mini pizzas

1 Make the tomato base

Chop and fry the onion in oil for 5 minutes. Add the garlic and cook for 1 minute. Then stir in the tomato puree, ketchup, and water.

The pittas are easier to split if warmed a little first.

2 Split the pittas

Split the pittas in half and toast lightly until crisp. Divide the tomato base between the pittas and spread out right to the edges.

3 Add cheese

Ask an adult to help you grate the cheese. Scatter the cheese over the tomato base.

Preheat the grill to high

4 Now add topping

Choose your favourite toppings and place on top of the cheese. Try making a pattern or face.

Grill for 1-2 minutes until the cheese has melted

Cool slightly before eating

Toppings to try

ham

sweetcorn

olives, black, sliced ones

tomatoes, little cherry ones

peppers, green, yellow or red

spring onions, thinly sliced

15

Cherry tomato sauce

Sweet cherry tomatoes make a tasty sauce which is good with any pasta.

How to make it...

You will need:

- 2 tbsp olive oil
- 300g (10^{1}/$_{2}$ oz) cherry tomatoes
- 30g (1 oz) shallot (1 big shallot)
- 1 garlic clove
- 100g (3^{1}/$_{2}$ oz) passata
- 1 tbsp tomato puree
- 1 tbsp sun-dried tomato puree
- 50g (1^{2}/$_{3}$ oz) mascarpone
- fresh basil leaves (4–5 big leaves)

Makes 4 small portions
Preheat oven to 180°C/350°F/
Gas Mark 4

1 Prepare ingredients
Dice the shallot, crush the garlic, and measure out the tomato puree and passata.

2 Halve the tomatoes
Wash the tomatoes. Then cut in half lengthways and place on a baking tray lined with parchment.

3 Drizzle with oil
Drizzle 1 tbsp of the olive oil over the tomatoes. Then sprinkle with ^{1}/4 tsp salt. Now they are ready to roast.

Roast for 20-30 minutes

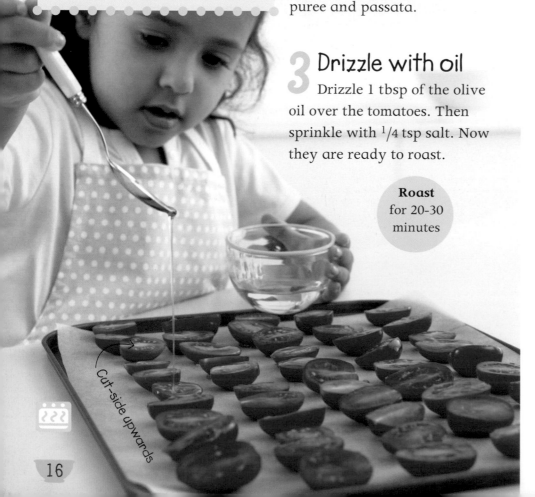

Cut-side upwards

4 Cook the shallot...
Cook the shallot gently in the remaining oil for 8 minutes, or until soft. Stir in the garlic and cook for another minute. Add passata, tomato purees, and roasted tomatoes. Bring to a simmer and cook for 10 minutes. Blend before you sieve.

5 Sieve the tomato mixture

Sieve the mixture over a bowl to remove the seeds and skins. You will need to press it through the sieve with a spoon.

6 Add the mascarpone

Blend the mascarpone into the sauce. Chop and stir in the basil leaves. You may want to add a little black pepper.

Try this!
Add strips of ham or halved black olives to the sauce.

Pour your tomato sauce over cooked spaghetti and mix in. Delicious!

17

Chicken dippers

You can vary this by using your favourite flavoured crisps for the coating.

How to make them...

You will need:

• 250g (9 oz) chicken breast

For the marinade
• 200ml (7fl oz) buttermilk
• 1 tsp Worcestershire sauce
• 1 tsp soy sauce
• 1 small clove garlic, crushed
• $\frac{1}{4}$ tsp paprika
• $\frac{1}{4}$ tsp dried oregano

For the coating
• 150g (5 oz) bag cheese-flavoured crisps
• 5 tbsp grated Parmesan cheese
• 6 tbsp plain flour
• 1 egg

Makes enough for 4 people
Bake at 200˚C/400˚F/Gas Mark 6

1 Make the marinade
Put the ingredients for the marinade in a large bowl and stir together until well mixed.

Wash hands after this

2 Cover the chicken
Cut the chicken into thin slices and mix into the marinade. Cover and leave for at least an hour.

3 Crush the crisps
Put the crisps in a large bag and scrunch with your fingers, until they become small crumbs. Pour the crumbs onto a large plate and mix in the Parmesan.

4 Flour, then egg, then crumbs
Put the flour on a plate and mix in a little pepper. Beat the egg in a bowl with a tablespoon of cold water. Dip the chicken in flour, egg, then crumbs.

5 Put on a baking tray

Put onto a baking sheet (no need to grease) and repeat until all the chicken strips are coated in crumbs. Bake in the oven for 15 minutes. Now wash your hands thoroughly.

Meanwhile...

6 Make some dips

Mix the ingredients for each sauce in a small bowl, ready to dip your cooked crunchy chicken in.

Bake for approx 15 minutes. Turn the chicken over halfway through the cooking time.

Allow to cool slightly before eating

Slightly spicy tomato

- 1/2 tsp sweet chilli sauce
- 2 tbsp tomato ketchup
- 2 tsp lime juice

Maple mustard mayo

- 4 tbsp mayonnaise
- 1 tsp wholegrain Dijon mustard
- 1 1/2 tsp maple syrup or honey
- 1 tsp cold water

To marinade: 10 minutes   To make: 35 minutes   To grill: 10 minutes

Chicken satay skewers

You could also make this with prawns (2 large raw prawns per skewer) or strips of beef.

You will need:

- 2 chicken breasts

For the marinade
- small piece of ginger
- 1 clove garlic
- juice of 1 lime (1 tsp reserved for sauce)
- 1 tbsp soy sauce
- 1 tbsp runny honey
- 1 tsp peanut butter (smooth)

For the sauce
- 100g (3^{1}/$_{2}$ oz) peanut butter (crunchy)
- 75ml (2^{1}/$_{2}$ fl oz) coconut milk
- 75ml (2^{1}/$_{2}$ fl oz) water
- 1 tbsp sweet chilli sauce
- 1 tsp soy sauce

Makes 10 skewers

Soak the skewers in water for 30 minutes to stop them from going black when you grill them.

How to make them...

1 Mix the marinade
Peel and grate the ginger (^{1}/4 tsp), crush the garlic, and put in a bowl along with the lime juice, soy sauce, honey, and peanut butter. Whisk together.

2 Bash the chicken
Put the chicken breasts in a sealable plastic bag. Use a mallet or a rolling pin to bash the chicken breasts until they are about ^{1}/2 cm (^{1}/4 in) thick.

3 Marinade the chicken

Slice each chicken breast into 5 strips and toss in the marinade. Leave for 10 minutes. Wash your hands.

Preheat the grill to high

4 Make the satay sauce

Meanwhile, make the sauce. Put the peanut butter, coconut milk, water, sweet chilli sauce, and soy sauce in a small pan. Warm gently, stirring constantly, until everything has melted. Simmer for 1-2 minutes until the sauce thickens. Remove from the heat, then stir in 1 tsp of the leftover lime juice and set aside.

Dip the chicken in the sauce

5 Thread and cook the chicken

Thread the chicken strips onto skewers and put on a foil-lined baking sheet. Wash your hands well. Grill for 5 minutes, then turn and grill for another 5 minutes until the chicken is cooked through.

Salmon fishcakes

These delicious little fishcakes will be swimming off your plate in no time.

How to make them...

You will need:

- 1 x 213g (7 oz) tin pink salmon
- 2 medium spring onions
- 2 tsp lemon juice
- $^1/_2$ tbsp mayonnaise
- $^1/_2$ tbsp tomato ketchup
- 40g (1$^1/_2$ oz) fresh breadcrumbs
- 2 tbsp plain flour
- 1 egg (medium)
- 50g (1$^1/_2$ oz) dried breadcrumbs
- 2 tbsp sunflower oil

For the dip
- 2 tbsp mayonnaise
- 1 tsp lemon juice
- 1 tsp sweet chilli sauce

Makes 6 fishcakes

To make breadcrumbs: Blitz 2 slices of white bread (without crusts) in a food processor.

1 Flake, add, mix

Drain the liquid from the salmon, then put the salmon in a bowl. Remove the skin and bones and mash lightly. Chop and add the spring onions. Add lemon juice, mayonnaise, and ketchup and mix it all up.

2 Divide it up

Add the fresh breadcrumbs, then mix again. Divide the mixture into 6 and form into balls, pressing firmly together. Then gently flatten into round patties. Ask an adult to make some of these fish-shaped.

4 Finish and cook

On the fish-shaped fishcakes make a space for the eye with your little finger. Heat the oil in a non-stick frying pan and fry the fishcakes over a medium-high heat for 1¹/₂ minutes each side, until they turn golden. Blot on kitchen towel and cool slightly. Add a cooked, frozen pea for each eye.

3 Dip in flour, egg, then breadcrumbs

Put the flour on a plate. Beat the egg in a shallow dish and put the dried breadcrumbs on another plate. Take each fishcake, dust it with flour, then dip it in egg and coat with breadcrumbs. Wash your hands.

Sweet chilli dip

While the fishcakes cool, mix the dip ingredients together in a small bowl.

You can serve these with a few chips or simply on their own with the dipping sauce

Corn quesadillas

These make a super-tasty, quick supper.
They will soon become a favourite dish!

You will need:

- 1 tbsp olive oil
- 1 small red onion
- $1/2$ red or orange pepper
- 1 x 198g (7 oz) tin sweetcorn
- 1 tbsp balsamic vinegar
- 1 tbsp runny honey
- 4-5 flour or corn tortillas
- 4 heaped tbsp salsa
- 100g ($3^1/2$ oz) Cheddar cheese

Makes 4-5 quesadillas

You can use **mild or medium** salsa

How to make them...

1 Prepare ingredients

Chop up the red onion and the pepper, drain the sweetcorn, and grate the Cheddar cheese.

Did you know that quesadillas (pronounced ke-sah-dee-uh) are a Mexican dish?

2 Stir, stir, stir

Heat oil in a pan and stir-fry onion and pepper for 3 minutes. Add corn and cook for 2 minutes until the onion and pepper are soft. Add vinegar and honey–after 1 minute remove from heat.

3 Spread the mixture

Spread half of each tortilla with a heaped tbsp of salsa. Then add some of the corn mixture.

Preheat the grill to high

4 Sprinkle the cheese

Scatter a little cheese over the salsa and corn mixture. Make sure you don't use too much as you will need some cheese to put on top of each tortilla.

5 Roll and cook

Roll the tortillas up and put on a baking sheet. Scatter over the rest of the cheese. Grill the quesadillas for 1-2 minutes until the filling is hot and the cheese topping is lightly golden.

Have a cooking party

If you like cooking and you like having parties, why not do both at the same time? Invite a few friends and make some of your favourite recipes together.

Peanut butter bears

1 Put the Rice Krispies in a bowl and stir in the icing sugar and sesame seeds.

2 Melt the peanut butter and butter in a pan. Add to the bowl and stir in.

3 Divide the mixture into 8 and squish each portion together with your hands.

Cut-out Cookies

1 Beat the butter, sugar, vanilla essence, and egg together.

2 Sift in the flour and add the salt. Mix again to make a dough.

3 Press the dough together to make a ball.

4 Roll the dough out, then chill for 30 minutes.

5 Cut out shapes using cookie cutters.

Make some recipe cards

Ask an adult to write out the recipes. The steps need to be clear. You can help decorate the cards.

Use both sides of the recipe card.

What you need to do

1. **Decide how many people** are coming. It's good to work in pairs so go for even numbers.

2. **Choose your recipes**, then make a list of the ingredients you need.

3. **Borrow equipment** from friends if you do not have enough utensils, baking tins and trays etc.

4. **Make invitations** to post or give out to your friends.

5. **Make recipe cards** with easy steps to follow. You can read through the steps together before you start.

6. **Prepare the ingredients** before everyone arrives. You could measure them out into small bowls or plastic bags.

7. **Find volunteers** (maybe mums or dads) to help out on the day.

Please come to my
Cooking Party
Alfie

Create your own invitations

Tie tags to wooden spoons for your invitations and give these out to your friends. These can be simple squares of coloured paper or special cut-out shapes.

Tell your friends to bring their spoons to the party.

Attach the tags with colourful ribbons.

Cookie cutters come in lots of wonderful shapes. Draw an outline around them in pencil, then cut out and write your message.

Don't forget to take **photos** of your cooking **party!**

27

Party time!

Decorate a room for your party. When you've finished cooking you can sit down to eat your home-baked treats.

Which pizza was yours? Did it have a funny face?

Mini pizzas and cut-out cookies are party favourites and fun to make.

In between recipes or while your food is baking...

...or when you have finished eating, you can **play some games.**

Ready, steady, GO

Party games

Empty a few packets of Smarties into a large bowl. Use straws to suck up as many as you can in one minute. Put the ones you win on a plate or piece of paper.

Something to take home...

Party bags

When you have decorated your cookies and peanut butter bears put a few into little clear bags for your friends to take home and enjoy.

Multicoloured meringues

Choose any colours you like, but use the food colouring sparingly, one drop at a time.

How to make them...

You will need:

- 3 egg whites (*medium*)
- 150g (6 oz) caster sugar
- $^1/_2$ tsp cornflour
- $^1/_2$ tsp lemon juice
- Food colour – pink, green, orange
Use a cocktail stick (toothpick) to add one drop at a time.

Makes 30 meringues

Bake at 130°C/250°F/Gas Mark 1

1 Separate the eggs

Crack the eggs over a large bowl, keeping the whites only. Put the yolks in a smaller bowl and set aside (how to separate, see p 5).

2 Whisk the whites

Whisk the egg whites to stiff peaks. Be careful not to overbeat, as they will start to look lumpy, a bit like cotton wool (see p 5).

3 Add the sugar

Add one tbsp of sugar to the egg whites, whisk in, then add a second and whisk back to stiff peaks. Whisk in the rest of the sugar.

4 Add lemon juice...

Whisk in the cornflour and lemon juice until just combined. The meringue should look smooth and glossy.

5 Add a little colour

Divide the meringue into 3 bowls and colour each one with a couple of drops of food colouring. Fold the colour in using a spatula.

Piping tips:
To fill the piping bag stand it in a tall glass and fold the edges down over the rim.

For the swirls, use a 13mm (½ in) nozzle.

Serving suggestion

When the meringues are cool, sandwich them together with whipped cream or softened vanilla ice cream.

Make meringue swirls

Spoon the meringue into a piping bag and squeeze to make swirls onto 2 baking sheets lined with parchment. Make each one about $2^1/2$ cm (1 in) across. Now bake in the oven.

Try this...
Just swirl the food colouring through the meringues a bit to get a marbled effect

Bake the meringues for 30-35 minutes, until firm on the outside. Turn off the oven and leave them for a further 45 minutes. Remove from the oven and cool.

Tropical ice lollies

Make this refreshing frozen Pina Colada on a stick. It's delicious!

You will need:

- 1 x 432g (1 lb) tin crushed pineapple in natural juice
- 85g (3 oz) caster sugar
- 120ml (4 fl oz) coconut milk
- 1 large lime

Makes about 6-8 ice lollies

2 Add lime
Squeeze the lime and add 2 tbsp of juice to the mixture. Whizz again.

How to make them...

3 Fill the lolly moulds
Pour into ice-lolly moulds. Leave a little room at the top.

1 Put in a blender and whizz until smooth
Put the pineapple, sugar, and coconut milk in a blender.

4 Put the lids on...
...and add the lolly sticks.

Ready
for
the freezer

To remove the frozen lolly from the mould, run warm water over it.

Freeze until firm– at least **6 hours**, but best overnight

Make some mini ice pops

Pour some of the mixture into small ice-cube moulds (a rubbery type is best for easy removal). Freeze for around 2 hours, until almost firm. Insert small wooden skewers or cocktail sticks and freeze again until solid.

To make: 30 minutes To bake: 12-14 minutes

Mini banana muffins

These mini banana muffins are made with tasty wholesome ingredients. They are just perfect for little fingers.

How to make them...

You will need:

- 1 medium egg
- 1/2 tsp vanilla extract
- 55g (2 oz) soft light brown sugar
- 1 large, very ripe banana
- 55ml (2fl oz) sunflower oil
- 85g (3 oz) wholemeal flour
- 1/2 tsp baking powder
- 1/2 tsp bicarbonate soda
- 1/4 tsp ground cinnamon
- pinch salt

Makes 18 muffins

Preheat oven to 180°C/200°F/ Gas mark 4

1 Line the tins
Line 2 mini-muffin tins with 18 mini-muffin liners.

2 Mix egg and sugar
Crack the egg into a large bowl, then add the brown sugar.

3 Whisk together
Add the vanilla extract and beat together until thick.

4 Mash the banana
Break the banana into pieces in a small bowl, then mash it well with a fork.

5 Add to egg mixture
Add the mashed banana and the oil to the egg and sugar mixture.

6 Sieve the flour

Sift on the flour, baking powder, bicarbonate of soda, salt, and cinnamon. Add the bran left in the sieve to the bowl too. Stir together until just combined.

Store in an airtight box for up to 3 days.

Try this!

Add a slice of banana or a sprinkle of sugar to the top

Fill the muffin cases

Spoon into the muffin cases (around two-thirds full). Then bake.

Bake for 12–14 minutes until risen and firm

Peanut butter bears

Great for a Teddy Bear's picnic, teatime treat, or birthday party.

You will need:

- 40g (1$\frac{1}{2}$ oz) Rice Krispies
- 75g (2$\frac{1}{2}$ oz) icing sugar
- 2 tbsp sesame seeds
- 100g (3$\frac{1}{2}$ oz) smooth peanut butter
- 40g (1$\frac{1}{2}$ oz) unsalted butter

To decorate

- 16 chocolate buttons
- mini M&Ms
- black writing icing

Makes 8 bears

How to make them...

1 Add and stir

Put the Rice Krispies in a large bowl and stir in the icing sugar and sesame seeds.

2 Melt and mix

Melt the peanut butter and butter in a pan over a low heat. Pour the mixture into the bowl and stir until everything is well mixed together.

3 Make into patties

Divide the mixture into 8 parts (roughly 2 tbsp each), squish each one together with your hands, then roll into a ball. Put the balls on a baking sheet lined with parchment. Squish down slightly to flatten.

4 Decorate

Put chocolate buttons into the sides for ears and push in mini M&Ms for eyes and noses. Use the writing icing to draw mouths.

Chill in the fridge for 30 minutes or until firm

Cut-out cookies

It's fun to roll out dough and cut it into shapes.
Why not start a cookie-cutter collection?

How to make them...

You will need:

- 250g (8²/₃ oz) butter (room temp.)
- 140g (5 oz) caster sugar
- 1 egg yolk
- 2 tsp vanilla extract
- 300g (10¹/₂ oz) plain flour
- ¹/₄ tsp salt

Makes about 30 cookies

Bake at 180°C/350°F/Gas Mark 4

1 Start mixing

Put the butter, sugar, egg, and vanilla extract in a large bowl and beat together until well mixed.

2 Add the flour

Sift in the flour and add the salt. Mix again to make a dough.

3 Make into a ball

Now it's time to get sticky! Press the dough together firmly with your hands to make a ball.

Chill the rolled dough in the fridge for 30 mins

4 Roll out the dough

Roll the dough between a folded piece of baking parchment. until about 5mm (¹/₄ in) thick.

Turn the page for iced cookies

Press down firmly making sure the right side of the cutter is facing down.

5 Press out shapes

Cut out shapes using cookie cutters. Gather up the trimmings into a ball, then roll out again and make more shapes.

Mmm... freshly baked **cookies!**

Try this...

Make chocolate cookies by splitting the dough into two at step 3 and adding 1 tbsp cocoa powder to one half.

6 Put on a baking tray

Lift cookies with a palette knife and arrange the shapes slightly apart on non-stick baking trays.

Bake for about 14 minutes. Then cool on a rack.

Iced cookies

It's easy and fun to ice the cookies using tubes of writing icing. Choose your favourite colours.

Squeeze the tube gently and start decorating.

Try adding edible silver balls.

Artist's fruit palette and dips

Be creative – use lots of different fruits to dip in the delicious sauces!

Lemon yogurt

Mix together

- 3 tbsp Greek yoghurt
- 1 tsp milk
- 1 tsp icing sugar
- 1 tbsp lemon curd

Raspberry-vanilla

Mix together

- 85g (3 oz) raspberries (fresh or frozen and defrosted)
- $1^1/_2$ tbsp icing sugar
- 1 tbsp Greek yoghurt
- $^1/_2$ tsp lemon juice
- 2 drops vanilla extract

…with a hand blender. Then sieve to remove the seeds.

Tropical mango

Mix together

- $^1/_2$ large, ripe mango (125g/$4^1/_2$ oz cubed flesh)
- 1 tbsp tropical fruit juice
- 1 tbsp icing sugar

…with a hand blender. Sieve if the mango has lots of fibres.

Chocolate orange

- 1 orange
- 55g (2oz) chocolate (use milk chocolate, broken into small pieces)

Grate $^1/_4$ tsp orange peel into a bowl. Add 2 tbsp juice from the orange, then add the chocolate. Melt (see p 5).

Chop some fruit...

and get dipping!

Munchy oat bars

These oat bars are quick and easy to prepare, and they will give you loads of energy.

How to make them...

You will need:

- 80g (3¹/₂ oz) butter
- 80g (3¹/₂ oz) light brown sugar
- 60g (2¹/₂ oz) golden syrup
- 130g (4¹/₂ oz) oats
- ¹/₂ tsp salt
- 4 large dried apricots
- 35g (1¹/₂ oz) raisins
- 35g (1¹/₂ oz) dried cranberries
- 30g (1 oz) dessicated coconut
- 30g (1 oz) pecans or pumpkin seeds

Makes 8 bars (or 16 squares)

Bake at 180°C/350°F/Gas Mark 4

1 Melt the butter...
Put the butter, sugar and golden syrup into a saucepan and melt together over a low heat.

2 Add together
Put the rest of the ingredients in a large bowl. Snip the apricots with scissors, snap the pecan nuts.

3 Mix it all up

4 Add syrup mixture
Pour the warm butter and syrup mixture into the bowl.

5 Mix again
Now stir until everything is well mixed together.

Try different fruit and nuts in this recipe

6 Spoon into a baking tin

Line and grease a 20cm (8 in) square baking tin. Spoon the mixture into the tin and press down with a potato masher to level the surface. Now it's ready for the oven.

Bake in a preheated oven for 20 minutes.

Cut into bars or squares when cool, then store in an airtight container.

Mini lemon cheesecakes

These are so deliciously lemony, you might want to make double quantities!

You will need:

For the base
- 5 Digestive biscuits 70g (2 $^1/_2$ oz)
- 50g (1$^2/_3$ oz) butter

For the lemony topping
- 4 tbsp Greek yoghurt
- 6 tbsp lemon curd
- 1 tsp lemon juice
- 125ml (4$^1/_2$ fl oz) double cream

To garnish (optional)
- blueberries or raspberries
- icing sugar

Makes 4 cheesecakes in 7cm (2.8 in) wide, 3cm (1.2 in) deep ring moulds. Lightly oil the inside of the moulds.

How to make them...

1 Crush the biscuits
Put the biscuits in a plastic bag and crush them using a rolling pin.

Chill in the fridge while making the filling.

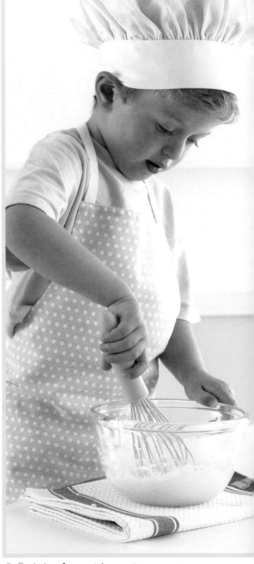

2 Melt the butter
Melt the butter in a small saucepan and stir into the crumbs.

3 Press into moulds
Divide the crumbs into a selection of ring moulds. Use clean fingers to press firmly into the base.

4 Make the topping
Put the yoghurt, lemon curd, and lemon juice into a large bowl and mix until smooth. In a smaller bowl, whip the cream until it makes slightly floppy peaks.

5 Fold in the cream

Mix 2 tablespoons of the whipped cream into the lemon yoghurt mixture, then fold in the remaining whipped cream.

6 Spoon into moulds

Spoon the lemon mixture carefully on top of the chilled biscuit bases. Fill to the top and smooth off with a palette knife.

Chill in the fridge for at least **30 minutes**, until firm

Garnish with blueberries and dust with icing sugar

Try lime... or orange curd instead of lemon curd.

Find out how to remove the ring mould on p 5.

Homemade lemonade

Refreshing on a hot day and packed with vitamin C.

How to make it...

1 Make the syrup
Put the sugar in a heatproof bowl and add the hot water. Stir to dissolve the sugar then set aside to cool.

You will need:

- 200g (7 oz) sugar
- 150ml (1/4 pint) hot water from the kettle
- 6 large lemons
- 850ml (1 1/2 pints) chilled still or sparkling water

Makes 1.25 litres (2 pints)

Try pink lemonade Just add a few drops of grenadine.

Try fruity ice cubes

Put blueberries and tiny sprigs of mint in ice cube trays. Fill with water and freeze.

Add lemon slices and mint

2 Roll the lemons
This helps release the juice.

3 Squeeze the lemons
You need 250ml (9fl oz) of juice.

4 Add sugar syrup and chilled water
Pour the juice into a jug and stir in the sugar syrup. Add the water.

Fruit skewers

Make traffic-light fruit skewers with scoops of different coloured melons.

How to make them...

You will need:

- 1 watermelon (red)
- 1 cantaloupe melon (orange)
- 1 honeydew melon (green)

1 Make melon balls
Cut the melons in half and use a melon scoop to make balls of different colours.

2 Put on straws
Push a straw through the middle of the balls of melon. Remember the order is red, then orange, then green.

47

Index

Annabel Karmel

Annabel is a leading author on cooking for children and has written 15 best selling books which are sold all over the world.

She is an expert in devising tasty and nutritious meals for children without the need to spend hours in the kitchen.

Annabel writes for many newspapers and magazines and appears frequently on radio and TV as the UK's expert on children's nutritional needs. She has her own range of healthy foods for children in supermarkets.

Annabel was awarded an MBE in 2006 in the Queen's Honours List for her outstanding work in the field of child nutrition.

Visit Annabel's website at **www.annabelkarmel.com**

Other children's titles written by Annabel
Children's First Cookbook 978-1-4053-0843-4

Acknowledgments

With thanks from Annabel to: Caroline Stearns, Marina Magpoc, Letty Catada, Evelyn Etkind and my children Nicholas, Lara, and Scarlett for testing the recipes with me.

Thanks to the models in this book:
Tiana Baily, Mia Basford, Theo Cadby, Alfie Cooke, Luella Disley, Leah Fatania, Jasmin-Rae Germaine, Samuel James, Maisie Kemplin, Fred Manns, William Nichols, Daniel Price, Lewis Shamplina-Posner, Millie Sheppard, and Jasmine Teal.

Thanks also to Howard Shooter for photography on pages 42-43 (step sequence).